JOHN LESLEY

THE WORLD'S GREATEST CITIES

LONDON

UNITED KINGDOM

REDBACK publishing

First published 2024 by
Redback Publishing
PO Box 357 Frenchs Forest NSW 2086
Australia

www.redbackpublishing.com
orders@redbackpublishing.com

ISBN 978-1-761400-74-2

Author: John Lesley
Editing: Caroline Thomas
Design: Redback Publishing

NATIONAL LIBRARY OF AUSTRALIA

A catalogue record for this book is available from the National Library of Australia

Original illustrations © Redback Publishing 2024
Originated by Redback Publishing

Acknowledgements
Abbreviations: l—left, r—right, b—bottom, t—top, c—centre, m—middle. We would like to thank the following for permission to reproduce photographs: Images © shutterstock; pg10br AndyScott, CC BY-SA 4.0 <https://creativecommons.org/licenses/by-sa/4.0>, via Wikimedia Commons, pg12 HeritageDaily, CC BY 3.0 <https://creativecommons.org/licenses/by/3.0>, via Wikimedia Commons, pg13tl Matt Brown, CC BY 2.0 <https://creativecommons.org/licenses/by/2.0>, via Wikimedia Commons, pg13bl Alla Tsyganova / Shutterstock.com, pg13br Ministry of Information Photo Division Photographer, Public domain, via Wikimedia Commons, pg14t Michael Ting / Shutterstock.com, pg14b Claudio Divizia / Shutterstock.com, pg15tr pio3 / Shutterstock.com, pg16-17 IR Stone / Shutterstock.com, pg19tr Peter Moulton / Shutterstock.com, pg22bl seancooneyfoto / Shutterstock.com, pg23t AR Pictures / Shutterstock.com, pg22br Pajor Pawel / Shutterstock.com, pg24bl Old Town Tourist / Shutterstock.com, pg25r Alex Segre / Shutterstock.com, pg25l Claudio Divizia / Shutterstock.com, pg29b Wirestock Creators / Shutterstock.com

CONTENTS

LONDON QUICK FACTS

London is the capital city of the United Kingdom (UK), which includes England, Northern Ireland, Scotland and Wales, plus a few small islands off the coast of the mainland. London is in the southeast of the United Kingdom.

At the heart of London, on the banks of the River Thames, is the City of London, which is also known as the 'Square Mile'. Spreading around this is Greater London, which includes 32 local government areas, called boroughs.

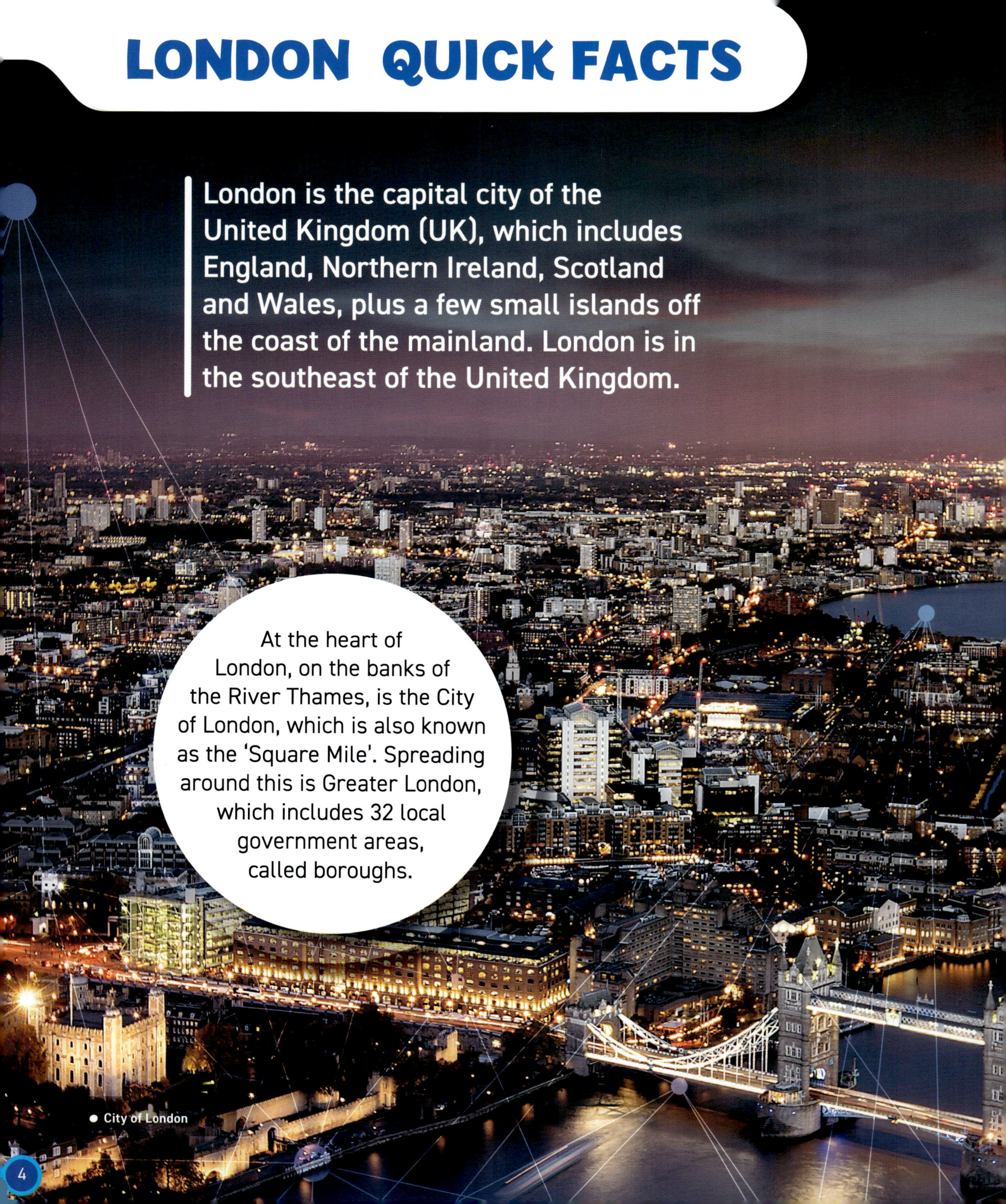

City of London

Greater London extends out over 1,500 square kilometres. In the past, the suburbs of Greater London were once villages and towns. As the population of London grew, these separate settlements were gradually absorbed into Greater London.

DID YOU KNOW?

London has over 20% of its area covered by trees. Without its urban infrastructure, this would class it as a forest, based on the United Nation's definition of the word.

LONDON'S GEOGRAPHY

London was developed on both sides of the River Thames, which was once much wider than it is today. Large parts of the swampy land along the original river banks have been reclaimed and engineered with foundations for buildings and public spaces.

SMOG

Smog, which is an unhealthy combination of fog and smoke, is a word that was invented to describe the London atmosphere over a hundred years ago. Smoke bellowing from chimneys on homes and factories once contributed to the smog, giving London some of the worst cases of air pollution anywhere in the world and causing countless deaths. Laws passed in the 1950s and 1960s to ban the burning of coal in London have led to a great improvement in air quality.

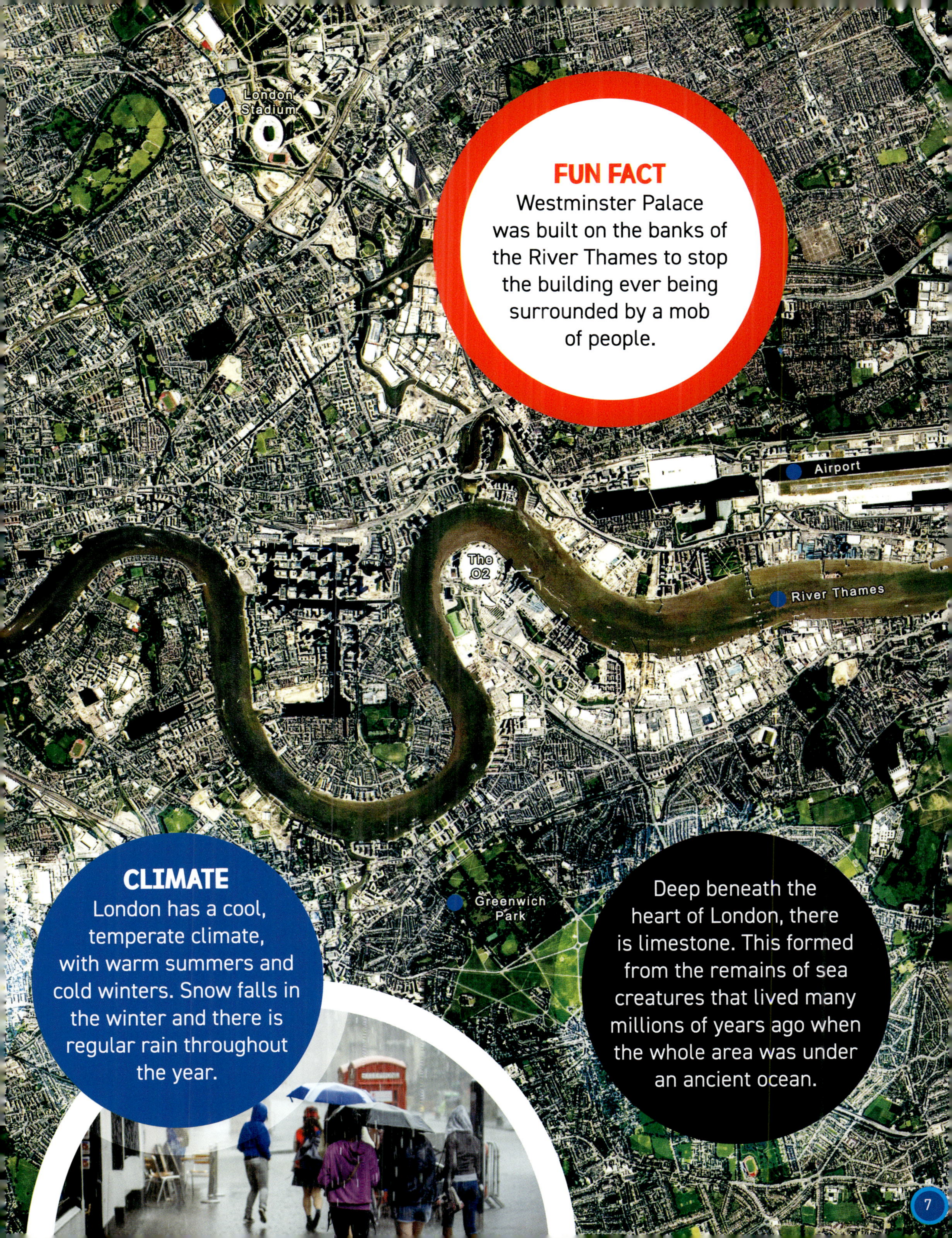

FUN FACT

Westminster Palace was built on the banks of the River Thames to stop the building ever being surrounded by a mob of people.

CLIMATE

London has a cool, temperate climate, with warm summers and cold winters. Snow falls in the winter and there is regular rain throughout the year.

Deep beneath the heart of London, there is limestone. This formed from the remains of sea creatures that lived many millions of years ago when the whole area was under an ancient ocean.

THE RIVER THAMES

The River Thames rises as a spring in the Cotswold Hills. It flows through southern England until it reaches London, before emptying into the North Sea at the Thames Estuary. The River Thames is over 340 kilometres long, making it the second-longest river in the UK.

The River Thames has been used as a source of water for drinking and for industries, a place to dump sewage, a highway for transport to and from London, and a recreation area where residents and tourists can enjoy boating and river sports.

FUN FACT

A raindrop that falls into the Thames in the Cotswolds will be drunk by eight people before it reaches the sea.

THE THAMES BARRIER

With so much of London being sited on the mostly flat plains that formed the original river banks, flooding has been a problem. The River Thames is subject to high tides and storm surges, and its waters used to flood large parts of London.

In 1984, the Thames Barrier was constructed downstream, a few kilometres from the London city centre. Ten huge steel gates span the river and are designed to be able to hold back water, to stop it from flowing across London. The gates are closed when high tides or storm surges threaten London with flooding.

● Thames Barrier in London

LONDON'S WATER SUPPLY

London is located on one of the drier parts of Britain, and most of the city's drinking water is drawn out of the River Thames. Some water also still comes from underground wells. Water authorities ensure the water is clean enough to drink, even though the River Thames is used as both a source of clean water and a place to dispose of treated sewage.

Wastewater treatment processing plant in North London

DID YOU KNOW?

The swans that live on the River Thames were introduced in the 12th Century by Richard the Lionheart – the English King who couldn't speak English!

In 2016, a London well that is at least 900 years old was discovered in the basement of Australia House, which is the location of the Australian High Commission in the UK.

FATBERGS IN LONDON'S SEWERS

It sounds unbelievable, but authorities in London constantly have to clear sewer blockages of solid fat and goo that are bigger than a bus! These disgusting 'fatbergs' threaten to block London's sewer system, the contents of which flow out into the River Thames after being cleaned in enormous wastewater treatment works.

Fatberg memorial manhole cover, Whitechapel

BRIDGES OF THE RIVER THAMES

Tower Bridge is an historic bridge that is recognised around the world as a symbol of London. It dates from the late 1800s and has a deck that can open to allow ships to pass.

FUN FACT

Albert Gunter once jumped his double-decker bus over Tower Bridge! He was driving over the bridge in 1952, when it began to open! He put his foot on the accelerator and managed to jump over to the other side! He got a day off work and £10 for his bravery!

The Millennium Bridge opened for pedestrians in 2000 but was immediately closed for repairs when it started swaying dramatically. This bridge appears in one of the *Harry Potter* movies, where it is destroyed by the Death Eaters.

There are many tunnels bored underneath the River Thames. One of them dates from the 1840s, making it the first traffic tunnel built under a river anywhere in the world.

LONDON'S HISTORY

Some ancient Celtic structures around London may be over 6,000 years old, but the beginnings of the city date from the Roman invasion of Britain, which was begun by Julius Caesar in 55 BC.

The Romans founded a city called Londinium on the banks of the River Thames. Many of London's main roads still follow the old Roman roads that date from around 2,000 years ago.

London was later invaded by various other groups, including the Vikings, and was conquered by the Normans, led by William the Conqueror in 1066.

London grew to be the centre of the whole British Empire, one of the most powerful and wealthy in human history.

- Londinium was a settlement established on the current site of the City of London around AD 43

BREXIT

Britain's withdrawal from the European Union (EU) in 2020 was called Brexit (short for 'Britain's Exit' from the EU). This change continues to impact the United Kingdom in a variety of ways.

FIRE AND DISEASE

London's early buildings were mostly made from timber. When a fire broke out in a bakery in 1666, the Great Fire of London began, destroying a huge part of the city.

London's population grew quickly, but the water supply remained unchanged. Water was drawn from wells with dirty water and in the 1800s a series of cholera outbreaks killed thousands of people. The threat of becoming sick was one of the reasons people wanted to escape London. A lucky few managed to emigrate to America, Australia and a range of other countries.

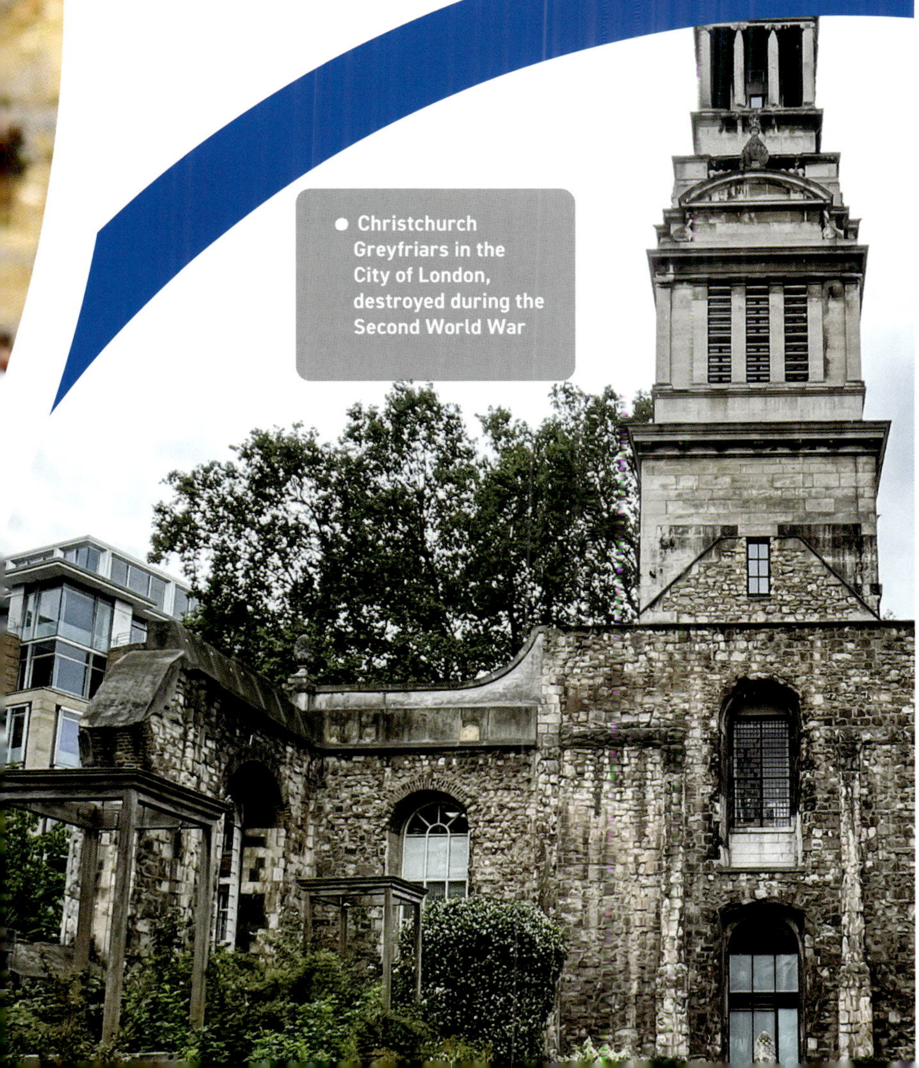

- Christchurch Greyfriars in the City of London, destroyed during the Second World War

SECOND WORLD WAR, 1939 TO 1945

During the Second World War, when Britain was at war with Germany, London was a main target for bombing by German fighter planes. Whole areas were levelled by the explosion of bombs and many people died. During this time, the underground railway stations were used as bomb shelters. Air-raid sirens would often sound at night and everyone nearby would have to go down into the tunnels to sleep in safety while bombs dropped above.

TRANSPORT IN LONDON

LONDON UNDERGROUND, 'THE TUBE'

London's underground railway system dates from the 1860s. It was the first to be built underground anywhere in the world.

The map of the Underground was created in the 1930s using a radical new idea in map design. It has been the basis of many other cities' railway maps, including the ones for Sydney and Melbourne. The map does not follow the actual shape of the railway lines. Instead, it clearly shows how all the stations are connected.

LONDON CABBIES

London's cabbies, or taxi drivers, are famed for their knowledge of all the tiny, twisting streets of the city. Before being allowed to operate a London taxi cab, a person has to pass a test to prove he or she has 'The Knowledge' of how to drive to any destination in London. Some people devote years of study to learn thousands of London streets before passing the test.

RED BUSES

The red, double-decker buses of London date from the mid-1900s. They have been updated since then, but tourists still love to take a ride on one of the older red buses, some of which have an open top for sightseers.

LONDON'S PEOPLE

POPULATION

With a population of around nine million people, Greater London is the United Kingdom's largest metropolis. The central part of London, the City of London, has a population of less than ten thousand.

FUN FACT

The City of London is the smallest city in England, yet over 300 languages are spoken there!

London has a large proportion of people who have come to live there from overseas, or whose ancestors were born overseas. It is the most ethnically diverse area in the UK. Ever since the time of the Romans, 2,000 years ago, London has been a city that has attracted residents and visitors from many different countries.

RICH AND POOR

The Industrial Revolution of the mid-1800s led to many farm workers losing their jobs, as machines took over the tasks they used to do. Thousands of people moved to London looking for work of any sort. This resulted in the growth of slum areas to house them. Many of these small houses have now become desirable homes for modern Londoners.

British society still has a class system, including people from the aristocratic upper classes, the middle classes and the poorer lower classes.

CELTS, ROMANS AND NORMANS

There were prehistoric Celtic people living in the south of England when the Romans invaded and began building Londinium. The Romans sent people to settle in England 2,000 years ago, and they brought with them a society whose wealth was dependent on having a constant supply of slaves to do work without any pay.

The Normans, who came from northwest France, invaded England in 1066. They made Westminster in London their capital city, and were responsible for building hundreds of castles throughout England to defend the land they had conquered.

Remains of the Norman Kidwelly Castle Carmarthenshire Wales

GOING TO SCHOOL IN LONDON

Primary and high school education for children in London is compulsory for ages 5 to 18. Most children go to school, but a few are home-schooled.

Students who want to undertake tertiary education after leaving school work towards achieving the General Certificate of Education (GCE) A-Level in their final two years of schooling.

- Cambridge University, London.

There are both public and state schools in London. State schools are run by the UK government, while public schools are privately owned and operated.

London's public schools include some of the oldest in the Western world. Their style of operation influenced the development of private schools in other parts of the world, with their emphasis on team sports and the importance of wearing uniforms.

WILDLIFE IN LONDON

Although London is a busy city with a large population of people, wildlife thrives in this urban forest. London has large areas devoted to parks and natural, open spaces. Gardens around houses, land beside railway tracks, and any vacant or unused land are important habitats for London's wildlife. These areas are havens for the native animals that make their home in the middle of one of the world's major cities.

FOXES

Foxes are a much loved native animal in London. These clever and adaptable creatures manage to thrive right in the centre of London.

MOLES

Moles are small animals with black fur, tiny eyes and front paws designed for digging. They live underground, eating worms and grubs. Their eyesight is not well developed but their sense of smell is excellent. A mole will leave small piles of soil as they tunnel beneath lawns and gardens.

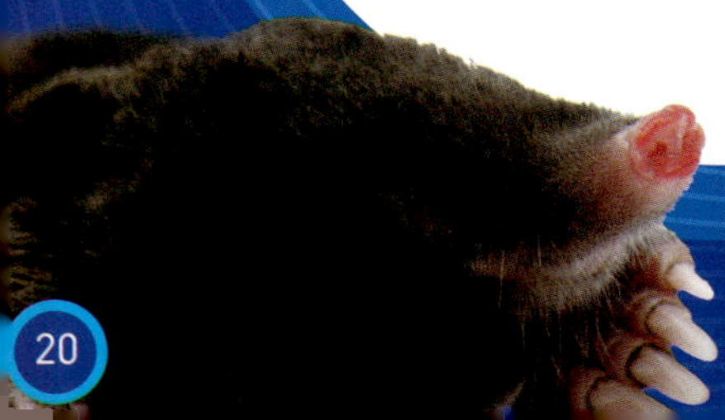

PEREGRINE FALCONS

These beautiful little falcons are birds of prey that hunt small animals and birds. The peregrine falcons now sometimes build their nests on London's tall buildings.

FUN FACT

London has almost as many trees as people!

BADGERS

The black and white badger grows to be about as big as a small dog. They live in burrows called setts, with lots of rooms for all the family!

HEDGEHOGS

These spiky little mammals have soft, smooth bellies that allow them to curl into a tight, spiky ball to protect themselves. They are great swimmers and can also climb trees!

BUCKINGHAM PALACE

Buckingham Palace is the official London residence of the Monarch. As well as having private apartments, the palace has offices and areas for meetings and public events. It has had this role since 1837, when Queen Victoria became the Monarch.

FUN FACTS

The Changing of the Guard is an official guard change ceremony involving the five regiments of Foot Guards in the British Army. Their fur hat is made from the skin of black bears from Canada.

THE LONDON EYE

The London Eye takes the idea of a Ferris Wheel to new heights!

The London Eye is one of the biggest observation wheels in the world. Since its opening in 2020, it has become a popular tourist attraction. The views it offers across London are astounding

ST PAUL'S CATHEDRAL

There has been a church on the same site for 1,400 years, but the current St Paul's Cathedral dates from after the Great Fire of London. The ruins of the old church were replaced in the early 1700s, based on a design by Christopher Wren. The church is noted for its large dome, which includes the Whispering Gallery, where a person who whispers against the wall on one side of the dome can be heard clearly right over on the other side. Thousands of tourists to London have climbed all the way up to the dome just to try whispering against its inner wall.

FAST FACT

To stop the heavy stone cathedral from sinking into the marshy clay of London, it was built on a huge foundation of crypts that house the remains of kings and many other historical figures.

BRITISH MUSEUM

The British Museum is renowned worldwide for its collection of treasures from the ancient world. Egyptian mummies and remarkable household items from thousands of years ago, ancient Roman jewellery and sculpture, as well as prehistoric pots and weapons, are all just a few of the many items on display.

The British Museum is also famously the location where the Rosetta Stone is kept. This wonderful archaeological find was carved 2,000 years ago. The words in multiple languages carved into the stone helped scholars to translate Egyptian hieroglyphic texts that had previously been a mystery to them.

UNESCO WORLD HERITAGE SITES IN LONDON

HOUSES OF PARLIAMENT AND WESTMINSTER ABBEY

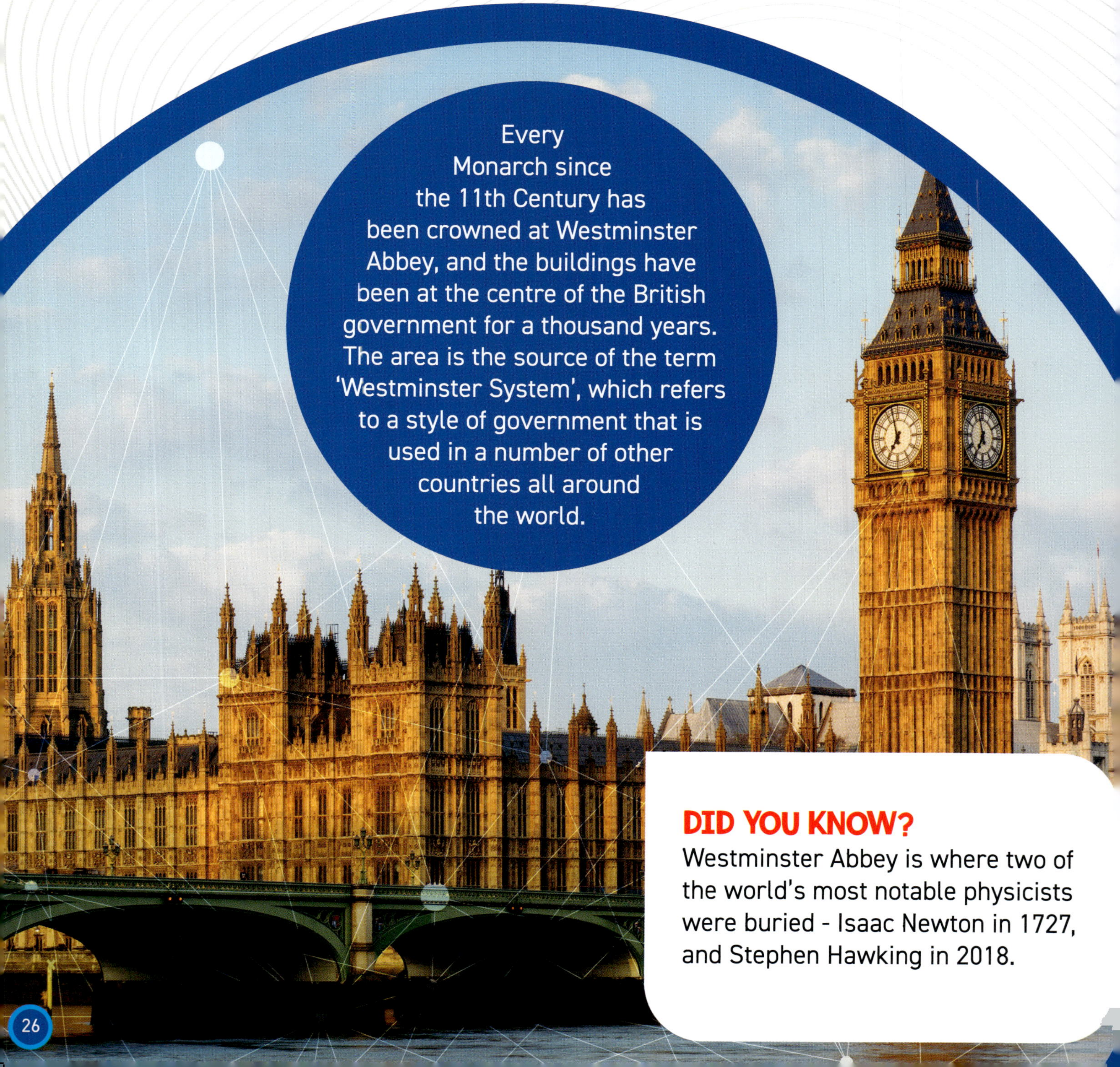

Every Monarch since the 11th Century has been crowned at Westminster Abbey, and the buildings have been at the centre of the British government for a thousand years. The area is the source of the term 'Westminster System', which refers to a style of government that is used in a number of other countries all around the world.

DID YOU KNOW?

Westminster Abbey is where two of the world's most notable physicists were buried - Isaac Newton in 1727, and Stephen Hawking in 2018.

TOWER OF LONDON

This building on the banks of the River Thames was begun as a fortress by William the Conqueror in 1066 after invading England. It was the tallest building in London right up until the 1800s. Over the years, it has been a palace, a jail and a tourist attraction. The Tower is the place where the Crown Jewels are kept. It is also the location where King Henry VIII had two of his wives executed in the 1500s.

FUN FACT

The Tower of London Was London's First Zoo! Between the 1200s and 1835, a range of wild and exotic animals were gifted to the Kings and Queens of Britain. They included leopards, lions, tigers, monkeys, elephants, zebras, alligators, kangaroos and even a polar bear!

Dating from the mid-1700s, Kew has been building its collection of world plants for over 250 years. The living collections there include over 30,000 different kinds of plants from all around the world. The herbarium is one of the largest in the world, with over seven million preserved plant specimens.

FUN FACT

During construction of the Princess of Wales Conservatory in 1985, Sir David Attenborough buried a time capsule in its foundations. The capsule contains seeds of important food crops and endangered species, and will be opened in 2085. By then, many of those plants may be rare or extinct.

MARITIME GREENWICH

FUN FACT
Before the Royal Observatory was built, there was no universal way of keeping time across the globe. Today, GMT or Greenwich Mean Time is the Universal Time that everyone uses all over the world.

This complex of buildings dates from the 1600s. They include the Royal Observatory, which is the place from which international time and all the world's lines of longitude are measured.

LONDON IN THE FUTURE

Government and community organisations are all working towards planning for London's future. Some of the projects they are working on will address providing for the future needs of Londoners in terms of transport, open spaces, housing and education.

THE ENVIRONMENT

Keeping the air, water and land clean and safe for Londoners will be a focus in the future. This will include looking at the level of carbon emissions, how to make electric vehicles the car of choice, and keeping open spaces, while still providing for a population that will increase by two million people over the next thirty years.

GLOSSARY

bellow (smoke) appear in large cloudlike quantities

borough local government area

Celtic referring to the indigenous people of Britain

cholera disease causing illness and often death

fatberg huge lump of fat in a sewer

fortress building that protects the area around it

haven place of safety

hub central place

limestone white rock made from the ancient bodies of tiny sea creatures

mainland larger part of a country, which has smaller islands offshore

reclaim fill in a water-covered area to make it dry land

renowned known widely for something positive

sewage contents of toilets

smog combination of fog and smoke in the air

spring (river) water coming from the ground where a river begins

temperate climate climate with mild summers and cool winters

INDEX